Saturday Night Mulberries
By Dorothy Ferguson

The first time
I remember crying
after my dad's death
happened the next year at school.

Someone in my class asked why I didn't have a dad.
Other kids were there, too, and they asked me where he was.

I told them he was dead.

I could feel a lump swelling up in my throat,
and it was hard to talk.
Someone asked, "What is dead?"

And I cried in front of them.
I cried there at school.

Another time,
we made presents for our parents.
All the kids in my class made one for their dads.
I didn't have a dad to make one for.
I cried right there at school. Again.

Once, the next spring,
I heard my big brother talking to my mom after supper.
He was really sad.
He told her the guys at school had been talking
about doing field work,
and getting the soil ready to plant the Spring seeds.
They would be working with their dads.
My brother was really feeling lonesome for our dad.
I heard him crying that night.

In the summer I would look up at the stars, or on stormy nights
I would hear the thunder, and see the lightning.

And it wasn't as neat as it used to be.
Without him there, the storms were scary.
I remembered how he would hold me up high
next to him, out there on the front porch.

And I really wanted him back.
It was hard to sleep.

D1360198

AN EDUCATOR'S GUIDE

by Majel Gliko-Braden

Illustration and Design
by Ron Boldt

Copyright ©1992
Revised 2004
A Centering Corporation Resource
All Rights Reserved.

ISBN: 1-56123-047-2

Additional copies may be ordered from:

Centering Corporation
PO Box 4600
Omaha, NE 68104
Phone: 402-553-1200
Fax: 402-553-0507

www.centering.org

Grief comes to class – your class. It's always uninvited, yet it marches in, takes a seat in the front row and defies you to ignore it. It disrupts your class, bothers the students and makes you feel helpless. Unfortunately, whether you're a first-year teacher or one who has taught for more than 20 years, you will at some time become acquainted with this unwelcome visitor. Grief just goes with the territory.

A tremendous amount of a young person's life is spent in your class and the school in general. By the time students are 18 years old, they will have spent 12 to 13 years in school, nearly 10 out of 12 months per year, 5 out of 7 days per week, and 6 of their most alert hours per day. The time students spend with teachers and classmates is more than they spend at home. You become a very important part of their lives.

Schools have become highly specialized. There are teachers for the developmentally disabled, learning impaired, emotionally disturbed, and physically handicapped. There are no special teachers for grief, but grief is in the classroom every day.

In 1976, 3.5 million children in the U.S. under the age of 19 lost one or both parents to death (Koch, 1977). The National Association of Elementary School Principals (1985) stated that by the time they reach 18, five children out of 100 will have had a parent die. Far more students will have had a grandparent, sibling, relative or close friend die.

When children experience the death of a grandparent, parent, sibling or any loved person, grief can be active in their lives for a long time. At first, supportive friends and relatives are there for bereaved children. Later on, you and other teachers or school counselors may become the ones to whom grieving children turn as they attempt to restructure their lives.

This book is the result of a study done through the College of Education at Montana State University, Bozeman. We focused on two areas related to the role of the educator with grieving students: 1. a survey of teachers was conducted to obtain perceptions and feelings about bereaved students and 2. interviews were held with bereaved students, K-12, along with parents and the teachers of these students at the time of the family member's death.

Tears and pain were shared during the interviews. Educators expressed their fears and inadequacies candidly. A cry for help was issued by both teachers and parents as they attempted to help their bereaved child/student. We hope that in some way, this little book does its part to answer that cry.

Majel Gliko-Braden

A View of History

Student:	When I see her locker with all her things in it, I cry.
Parent:	I dreaded them going back to school, having to face those kids and wondering what the teachers would say.
Teacher:	It's very painful; death in a student's family has been the most difficult problem I have ever handled in my 30 years in education.

Within this half-century, death in the family has changed for American students. Years ago death and dying were viewed as more natural parts of life. From infancy, children lived with the fact of death. School teachers were active with families socially and visited the homes of students. When death struck, they were part of the community which surrounded the family, helped with chores and meals, and shared in the funeral.

Bereaved students saw their teachers often, shared tears and mutual comfort. Michael Landon, in his series, *Little House On The Prairie*, more than once puts Laura in the position of helping a family through grief. In our fast-moving society, you as a teacher do not have this advantage.

You must deal with other factors: The physical distance of the family from extended family has affected how we grieve. It is less common for children to be raised around grandparents and other relatives. An annual visit may be the extent of a child's relationship with Grandma and Grandpa. The child is often denied learning a model of healthy grief from one's family. When the call comes informing the family of death, the student is taken to the place of bereavement where she observes grieving responses. This all happens with relatives and friends who are often friendly strangers.

Another distance factor exists. Often, the sick and dying are kept in hospitals and nursing homes. Visiting hours are posted and at times, children are not allowed. **Removing the sick and dying from their homes** has shown an effect on students. They feel isolated. Lack of exposure and experience to the dying process has created fears and inaccurate information. To most students death has become a monster to be feared and avoided.

In a class on bereavement for undergraduates, I asked, *How many of you have attended a funeral, wake, Shiva, or other death ritual?* Ten of 100 raised their hands. Most had never had the experience. They said fear kept them away. Others said family members discouraged attendance. They have missed life experiences that could have prepared them for later pain and grief.

All things change, life moves in cycles. Today some medical colleges are including classes in bereavement. The Hospice movement is alive and well in America and more and more people are learning about death, dying, and grief.

Environment, Culture and Personality ———————

Variables such as:

> a child's personality,
> experiences with death,
> the circumstances surrounding the death,
> a prolonged illness or a sudden death,
> the relationship a student has with self and family,
> ethnic-cultural background and
> family beliefs and rituals,
> are some factors affecting student bereavement.

Personality varies from child to child. Bereavement is as personal and individual as fingerprints. Generally, students who are quiet, non-talkative, and reserved grieve quietly. Those who are talkative and overt tend to be consistent with their personality. They may cry loudly and seem to be drawing attention to themselves.

Experiences with death vary greatly. Children who are able to ask questions about death, who have attended a funeral and received loving support have dealt with grief and life in a way different than those children who have taken their answers from television and movies.

Circumstances of the death have a tremendous affect. If a child is at home for some time with a dying parent, has time to say good-bye and understand what is happening, his grief will be different from that of a 10-year-old whose brother is murdered. The 10-year-old will have to deal with family rage, the justice system, multiple questions from friends and a very different kind of fear.

Prolonged illness offers both pain and opportunity. John and Tim received hospice support during their father's illness. The boys and their dying father used the time to talk about their fears, regrets, and concerns. When the death occurred, both boys felt their grief had been processed before the event. They did not experience the death as frightening, but as a relief of suffering for their dad.

Sudden death means grief work must be done after the death. Anna was a college freshman when her brother was killed. When the news reached her father, he died of a heart attack. Anna left school to attend both funerals, then returned to class. Soon a second brother was killed in a boating accident. Again, she went home for the funeral. She returned to school and explained to one of her professors. He said, *Now, I've heard many excuses from students for why they missed classes, but this has got to top them all.* Anna heard other unfeeling remarks from classmates. She dropped out of school and returned home. When I met Anna, she had once again returned to the university after a one-year absence.

Relationships with self and family play a part. One of the great writers on grief, Earl Grollman, tells a delightful story of a kindergartner whose grandfather died. The family was concerned because the little boy didn't seem to understand that Papa was gone, he wasn't grieving. Finally, Rabbi Grollman said, *It must be awfully sad to have your Papa die.* To which the boy said, *I only met him twice and both times he had bad breath.*

Cultural background influences grief reactions. Different cultures have different rituals for expressing bereavement. Some Irish-American families view death as a transition from this life to life with God. When someone dies, the family becomes involved with the preparation of the body. During the wake, family members celebrate the final stage of this life with their deceased. They celebrate with a meal and praying. Some openly state feelings and memories of their relationship with the deceased, such as, I'll never forget the time you. . . Laughter and crying are frequent. Children participate and learn grief patterns associated with their heritage.

Catherine told of her first experience with death as a small child. She said, **When a relative died it was common for children to touch the body.** Her tradition recognized that she was a part of the family who helped prepare the body. She recalls it as being positive and the thing to do.

Each culture has traditions of death rituals rooted through the passing of many generations. Some of these rituals are retained and involve children. Others have been discarded and not replaced. This can affect the responses of grief in children since they do not know that grief can be a healthy response to death.

Another factor in cultural background includes **belief systems**. These can be an asset to a grieving child. Three students shared how their religious beliefs helped them cope. They had been taught that when someone dies, the surviving family will see them again in a new world. The way the mother taught this faith principle gave the family comfort in believing they will see their father again.

On the other hand, one must be careful in teaching children religious concepts that may lead to fear and anxiety. Some children hear, **"Daddy's happy being with God"** as saying **"Daddy wasn't happy with them."**

All of these factors and differences come together when grief enters your classroom. In many cases, you may be the one key to normalcy with them. Death happens, and school goes on.

Developmental Changes ─────────────────────────

A child's age may well influence how that child reacts to death and how she grieves. However, developmental stages are merely a framework for understanding children's bereavement. As you well know, every child is individual and unique. Just because a child is a certain age does not mean she will react and respond a particular way.

Children give death a lot of thought. Being the newest of human beings, they are excited about tasting, touching, smelling, seeing and feeling life. They are unconcerned about all the complexities of the adult world. They see things simply and concretely, and they view death from these eyes, too.

1-3 Years: Death is no different from life. They cannot imagine anything so different from their own state of being.
They see life in death since they are alive and think of the whole world as being alive, too.
They see death as temporary and reversible, like sleep.
They cannot think of death as permanent.
Separation fear and fear of abandonment are common.

Maria's youngest child was two years old when her husband died. The family had an open-casket funeral. While the clergyman was addressing the congregation, her son announced that he was going to take a nap with his daddy. He hopped from Maria's lap, dashed to the casket and climbed in next to his father.

3-5 Years: Children seem unconcerned with death.
There is very little comprehension that death is permanent.
Death is still temporary to them.
Gone now-back later.
The dead are seen as having consciousness.
Death is seen as an accident and avoidable rather than inevitable.
There is fear of separation and worry that death is punishment.

Even helpful attempts to teach about death at this age may meet interesting responses. Sara was a teacher who had developed a program on children's concepts. While digging in her flower bed, she unearthed the remains of a dead rabbit. Wanting to practice what she preached, Sara called her 4-year-old daughter over. **Kayla**, she said, **this is a dead rabbit**. Kayla looked at the rabbit, turned to her Mom and said, **Well, cover it up then**.

5-8 Years: Now children begin to see death as permanent. They talk about being sad and afraid.
They become afraid of their own death and their parents'.
Death is seen as scary, cruel and dangerous. They begin to accept it, but try to keep it distant, to hide from it.
They wonder if thoughts and actions can cause it.
They want details of deaths, burial, traditions and survival tactics.

Jean's mother died when she was 8 years old. She and her mother had a tiff about Jean's messy bedroom. Jean refused to clean her room as her mother wanted, so her mother proceeded to clean it herself. Shortly after, her mother became ill and died. Jean's idea of her mother's illness and death was that her disobedient behavior killed her mom. It took years for Jean to accept that her behavior was not the cause of her mother's death.

8-10 years: While children know all living things do die, they still hold great hope that death will be delayed as long as possible. They are like most of us.
Death is seen as a video game monster and they know they can't win.
They feel sad, afraid and lonely.
Death is seen as a natural part of life, especially when the dying are old.

Ron's mother died when he was 10. The most helpful thing he remembers is a cousin coming into his room where he was lying, all alone, waiting for the word of her death. The cousin sat on his bed and began to list all the people who loved him. He joined in, and later began a game of chase through the house. As an adult, he has very little memory of that time.

From early adolescence through late teens, students usually understand that death is final. They realize that someday they too, will die. This growth stage can be challenging to teenagers as they develop their own thoughts and feelings about death and the meaning of life.

Bill, 17, is the oldest of 5 siblings. His father died at home following a long illness. Hospice volunteers helped the family. Bill decided to move a bedroll into his father's room and sleep beside his father's bed. He wanted to be the first caregiver when Dad needed something. The last ten months gave Bill and his dad time to talk about personal issues and feelings. After his father died, Bill's actions toward his brothers and sisters changed. Before, he was too involved with other interests to even bother with the family. After his experience helping his father, Bill redefined his views of life. He became interested in his sibling's activities and more involved with them.

A Separate Look At Teen Grief ———————————————

Sandy Priebe does extensive work with grieving teens in Alpena, Michigan. We asked her to pretend she was having a cup of coffee with you and share her thoughts. Sandy says:

"Teens have two grief behaviors, instant and delayed. Instant grief is seen in the break-up of a love relationship, not being picked for the team, a family divorce, death of a classmate, death of a grandparent. All these losses are directly related to the primary framework in which the emerging adult

identity is connected. Teens will display great outward emotion to these losses, and some even go so far as to attempt suicide.

If a classmate dies, teens will be very open. They will display a lot of emotion because they feel safe with their peers. They will mourn, grieve and memorialize as a group. They will pragmatically tell their parents their wishes should their own death occur. Teens deal with death in a business-like, bottom-line manner. They are still discovering self and need additional years to think about religious importance and deep questions. These usually crop up in late-night talk sessions after age 20.

If a teen has a parent or sibling die, grief will often be delayed. Nature has programmed the teen to survive major trauma so intellectual and emotional growth can continue. This delayed grief will stay dormant until the teen enters the early to mid 20's. A death of neighbor, pet, co-worker or even a news event can trigger these dormant feelings and grief can take place without personal destruction.

If a parent or sibling dies, have a card or flowers sent from your class. Explain that this communicates that the class is aware of the loss and will help remove the awkwardness students feel when the person returns. Remember that teens may well hate someone coming up and saying they are sorry. The teen wants to, above all, be normal. They are protective of their insulating shell and terrified of having that penetrated without their consent. If students write cards individually, be sure to explain who is absent so their missing name will not be taken as not caring.

Tell students who are friends that it is important to go to the funeral home. Tell them it is not necessary to say anything. Just showing up is important and a handshake or hug will say it all. They need not stay long or look at the body.

As their teacher, I suggest you treat your grieving teen students as you would a deer in the forest. Go gently, or it may leap and run away. Don't pry or give up-lifting advice. Let them know you are there for them, that they can talk to you at any time. Allow them the wisdom of what is in their best emotional interest.

Offer help with assignments if you feel they need it. Send a personal note, just from you, and visit the family at home or at the funeral home. And—if you are a teacher who becomes close to her students, you may be the person chosen as a sharing listener. If that is the case, you will have the unique privilege of listening, supporting and sharing. In any case, you'll find your major task will simply be to listen and be there.

It should be noted, too, that teens who have suffered a loss are at a higher risk of pregnancy. The need to be secure, to share, to break away from a sad household, all place them at higher risk. Our society limits intimacy between people. The role model of intimacy for teens is mostly media image and the model largely sexual. Both males and females who experience major losses seek out intimacy. One chaplain worked with boys who were arrested. She found 90% of them were grievers.

When grief strikes a teen, it is often a double whammy since adolescence itself can be a grief experience. It is the loss of a childhood, loss of comfort and the gradual leaving of a familiar household. Teachers have tremendous impact on teens, and supporting one during grief is extremely special."

What You Can Do To Help———————————————

First of all, help yourself:

Explore your own feelings and attitudes about death.
Attend inservices, local programs on death, visit with a grief counselor.

Understand the grief process.
Read some of the basic books listed at the end of this book.

Learn reactions of bereaved students and the affects on learning.
We include a separate section on this, other books have more.

Know the resources in your school and community.
Books, journals, professionals, counselors, ministers.

Express your care.
> Attend the memorial service.
> Call the student, parents.
> Make a home visit.
> Prepare or buy and deliver a treat the student likes.
> Express what you feel.

Saying you're sad may make more sense to children than saying you're sorry. The story on page 18, of Sue May and her student, John, shares an excellent sample of all of the above.

Create an atmosphere of openness and acceptance.
Respect the student's personal reactions to the death. Some children grieve more openly than others. In fact, your entire class may have spurts of questions and a variety of different feelings and concerns about their classmate.

Allow for reassurance.
If a grieving child, or even a classmate, needs more reassurance, allow a telephone call to visit with a parent.

Do not overprotect or be overly-permissive.
Include the student as you normally would. For some children this may be a welcome release from a sad household. School may be the only normal part of their lives.

Prepare and guide classmates before the student returns to school.

Children will want facts and honesty. They are usually eager to help and will have ideas about giving support.

Acknowledge the death.
Some teachers become frightened and ignore the grieving student. This gives the child a message of not caring. Express your sadness and concern. Show you care by a touch appropriate to the grade level—a hug, pat on the shoulder, etc.

Don't be afraid to ask for help.
Consult with the parents if you aren't sure what to do. Check with your school counselor. Be willing to modify your expectations.

Keep the parents or parent informed.
A simple phone call or a conference will be helpful.

Assign a student partner to aid the student with school work.
Usually this is a close friend who has the student's trust.

Listen.
Frequently this is the greatest gift you can give any griever.

Encourage grief expressions.
Your bereaved student may find freedom and support in talking, writing, drawing, through drama or through books and stories.

Deal with it openly.
Express your sorrow, sadness and concern to the family and your student.
This can be done through:

> a phone call to the family,
>
> a visit to the home,
> a written card.

No response can easily be seen as not caring. Grieving students who had teachers directly involved with their grief have said their return to school was more comfortable than those youngsters whose teachers showed no response.

Maria's father died when she was in kindergarten. After the death, her teacher never shared any concern and didn't speak with Maria about her grief. Maria felt no one at school cared about her daddy or her pain. The two most hurtful times at school were when classmates would tell about their weekends with their fathers or when a class project was made for parents. Her mother, Jane, asked the teacher how Maria was adjusting. The teacher said she had not talked to Maria because she didn't know what to say. She was afraid she would cause more hurt. After Jane's encouragement, the teacher talked with Maria about her father's death and Maria then felt her teacher cared.

Bridget's father died when she was in 4th grade. She felt her teacher was a true friend who cared and loved her throughout the school year. Her teacher first heard about the death from the principal. She had her students make cards and letters for Bridget. The same day, her teacher called the family, spoke with Bridget and an adult relative who invited her to the home. When the teacher got to the home, she hugged Bridget and delivered her classmate's cards, explaining who was absent and would be sending cards later. She assured Bridget of her care for her and told her not to worry about schoolwork right now. Bridget remembers seeing her teacher at the funeral. This made her feel truly loved. Now, in 9th grade, she still has contact with her old teacher.

Miss May and John

This simple, true story is an excellent example of caring and what to do.

It was Christmastime. Sue May was listening to the news driving home from school. She heard an accident had claimed the life of a local farmer, Toby Martin. Toby's son, John (10) was in her class. This was a small farming community and most folks knew each other. There were 21 students in her fifth grade class. Sue May sat in her car and thought, *What a horrible thing to happen at Christmas. I must call someone and see if this is true, then I'll call my principal.* She fought the bitter, blowing snow from her driveway to her house and began planning the conversations.

Hello, Mrs. Henry, this is Sue May, John Martin's teacher. When I was driving home from school I heard on the radio that Mr. Martin had been killed.

Yes, around noon today. My husband's over there now.

Immediately after that, Sue May called her principal.
Mr. Shook, this is Sue May, have you heard that Toby Martin was killed today?

Yes, I'll call Mrs. Martin tomorrow morning to see how I might be of help.

I'll call my student, John, and I'll tell my class tomorrow.

Sue began to plan the conversation with John. She was tense about talking to him, but her concern for this boy was important.

When the phone was answered at the Martin house she said, *Hello, this is Miss May, John's teacher. May I please speak with John or his mother?*

John's voice was shallow and soft. *Hello.*

Hi, John, this is Miss May. I wanted to call you to tell you how sad I am to hear about your father and I wanted to see how you are doing.

There are so many people over here that I don't know what's going on.

A lot of people love you and your family and they want to help. John, if you need to talk to someone about your feelings and what's happening, please tell me. I want to help too. Miss May promised to call John again the next day after school.

Miss May had anticipated a mood swing from her Christmas-anxious students. The next morning she faced a group of bewildered youngsters.

Good morning, she said. *Some of you may not have heard the sad news about the Martin family. Mr. Martin was killed in a car accident yesterday. Last evening I spoke with John on the phone. This is a very sad time for him, his family and friends.*

Different students began telling their facts about the accident and how their families were involved with helping the Martins. Miss May let the children share. Then she invited her class to talk about how they might help John during this tough time. Several ideas came up: go visit him, take him a gift, help with his schoolwork, play with him, write letters and cards. The rest of the morning the children were busy writing their letters and cards so their teacher could deliver them that afternoon.

During the rest of the day, the students made comments about John and when he would come back to school. Sue led a class conference about grief and how the class could help John. They decided on a buddy system where John's two best friends would move their desks near him and help him with his work. The other students would help by inviting John to play with them at recess and greet him the first day.

After school, Miss May spoke with her principal about how her class was becoming involved in supporting John. She mentioned delivering the cards and asked for someone to cover for her while she attended the funeral. The principal would send out notices to teachers and students saying students could attend the funeral with parental permission. Then Sue went to the teachers' lounge and called John.

Hi John, I told you I would call today. May I drop by with some cards and letters your class have made for you? She could hear John ask someone in the background. *My mom says that would be fine,* he answered.

Sue knew that John loved chocolate chip cookies, so on her way she stopped by the bakery and picked up a large decorated cookie that said, **To John. We care about you.**

When she arrived at his house, Sue was greeted by Mrs. Martin and John. She gently gave John a hug and took his mother's hands. She delivered the cards, letters and the cookie to John, talked with him a few minutes and assured him that she, along with several of his classmates, would be at the funeral.

Miss May attended the funeral, and when John came down the aisle at the end of the service, she gave him a smile and a wink. The family waited at the door while people expressed their sorrow. Sue had gotten a small present for John and gave it to him as she passed by. It was a wooden key ring with his name on it. After the service she returned to class.

Several students had questions about the funeral and what happens when someone dies. Miss May listened to the questions and the class discussion. She gave facts as best she understood them. When questions of religion arose, she encouraged students to ask their families what they thought. More than once she simply said, *I really don't know – what do you think?*

The next Monday, John returned to school with his mother. Miss May spoke with Mrs. Martin and John about the buddy system the students had arranged. She also assured Mrs. Martin that she would have a conference with her in three to four weeks to let her know how John was doing.

After his mother left, Miss May had a private talk with John at her desk before the other students began arriving. She offered to talk with John any time he needed to talk. If he wanted to talk with a school counselor, she would arrange that, too. As classmates began filing in, each took her/his turn welcoming John back, just as they had planned.

Sue May's story shows how helpful caring can be shared. Each of us has our own way to show how we care. What is most important is that we let our student know.

In some instances, you may want to involve the parents of your class. The following letter comes from another excellent resource, *Good Grief – Helping Groups of Children When A Friend Dies*. This book was written by Sandra Fox and produced by the New England Association for the Education of Young Children.

Dear Parents,

Today was a sad day for the High Street Day Care Center.
We learned of the death of Jimmy Hudson, one of the children
in our 4-year-old group. Jimmy died yesterday when he fell
through the ice on Bennett Pond and drowned.

Tomorrow morning we will be talking with the children about
Jimmy's death, giving them the information noted above. We
will be available to help with their questions and will be
thinking with them about a way to commemorate Jimmy's life.
Since they will also want to talk with you about what has
happened, we wanted to be sure you have information about it.

We would like to meet with as many parents as possible for a
few minutes tomorrow morning. We hope you will be able to
join us for a brief parent meeting from 7:30 to 8:00 am. Coffee
and muffins will be available for the adults and one of the
staff will have a light breakfast for the children who arrive
earlier than usual. If you will not be able to come to the
morning meeting, please feel free to call me at home this
evening (234-5678) if you would like to talk.

It is never easy to talk with children about something as sad
as the death of a child. I wish we could protect them from the
pain and grief associated with loss but in today's world, that
is not really possible. I believe the best thing we can do is to be
sure they have honest information – at a level they can understand and deal with – and that there are caring adults they
can talk with who will provide a sound beginning understanding for them about death and dying.

If you or your child would like to be in touch with Jimmy's family,
they may be reached at 666 Middle Street, (234-9876)

Sincerely,

When children see that adults are willing to answer questions, to talk about death and share honest information with them, their fears diminish and their trust increases. As the director says in her letter, we all wish we could protect and shelter children from the pain in the real world, but we cannot. Robert Cavanaugh, in an old book on death and dying called, *Facing Death*, says of children: *Volkswagons do the same job as Cadillacs. When their questions are answered, their feelings taken seriously and their anxieties addressed, children can handle grief as well as, if not better than, adults.*

In Times of Class Crisis

We've mentioned the death of a classmate. When that occurs the entire class is bereaved, frightened and uncertain of what to do. We asked two people to share what they did when a classmate died. Kathy Rocks is a counselor in Waynesboro, Pennsylvania.

"An 8th grade student was killed when the driver of the van in which she was riding lost control. She was pinned beneath the vehicle. Three friends were treated and released. The next day, one hour before school started, I met with the principals, guidance counselors and the director of pupil services. One-half hour later we met with the entire teaching staff. They were given information on how to respond to this crisis. We shared how the library would be used as a place for students to come to support and console each other and that the counselors would be available there to talk to students individually or in groups.

Some students learned of the death from others before school, others heard it for the first time from the principal over the public announcement system.

Students slowly filled the library as soon as they were given permission to do so. Some were sobbing, others were in shock and others were trying to understand. Many were looking for the first time at their own mortality. More than one student was angry, but most were saddened and horrified. They consoled each other in groups and occasionally would sit alone and grieve. As counselors, we allowed them their space but remained visible and available.

I approached groups slowly and listened to the feelings being expressed. I empathically responded and gave permission to share feelings and thoughts. Those who wanted to talk privately were taken to small offices. There the students shared feelings and memories. Many were surprised to learn that their current grief triggered unresolved grief from past losses. They told me of a grandfather's death, a friend's suicide, their parent's divorce and absent father. They told me how scary it was when they were in an accident. All this was a significant part of their grieving.

The students were very receptive to my presence and that of their counselors. They quickly trusted us. We continued to approach groups and to share. In looking back, I realize that had I waited for them to come to me, I would have sat alone. It was important that we reached out and encouraged them to talk.

To teachers, I would say STOP. Stop at the beginning of class if you sense the student's feelings about the death are overcoming their concentration. Give them the opportunity to talk about the death and how it has impacted their lives. Remember, you are modeling behavior for them, so you need to be aware of and comfortable with your own feelings about death.

LOOK. Look for an opportunity to let them know you care and are sad. Don't rush to remove or fill the empty chair of the dead student. It's okay to leave it vacant as a catalyst for sharing.

LISTEN. Listen to their feelings and listen to your own. Don't try to fix or control their feelings or take away their sadness. You cannot hurry the process. Each student will be on a personal time-table of grief. It's important to sense when they are ready to move on to class work. Getting back to normal is necessary for their well-being as well as for maintaining the continuity of education.

Keep communication open between you and the school counselor so you can encourage the students to work through their grief. This applies to any bereaved student in your class. And the basics for communication in grief are the old ones we first taught children when they crossed any street in life: Stop, Look, Listen."

Kathy ————————————————————————

A high school in Omaha, Nebraska, experienced the death of three students in one semester. The school counselors offered a grief group during the lunch hour. There were six sessions in which the groups heard from counselors, watched the *Family Ties* television show tape which dealt with the death of a friend and shared feelings. At the end of the six weeks students planned a trip to the cemetery where all three were buried. They had a memorial service, released balloons containing notes to their friends who had died, and were asked to evaluate the entire experience. This is what they said:

For myself it was good. I know I can finally be understood. I am so glad I had the chance to share my thoughts. It was the first time I told my experience to anyone and I feel at peace with the subject.

The group let me feel it was ok to cry and talk about death. I thought I was the only one who felt this way. I like talking to people like myself instead of a bunch of adults.

I said things mentally to her at her grave. I felt she could really hear me. When we let the balloons go, I thought it was like we were all sending her our love and thoughts.

I'm glad I went. It was good for us to see the graves and cry. I felt they were happy tears. I felt peace and I can look back on the memories without becoming emotionally distraught. I loved the balloons. I felt we were symbolizing our feelings about letting go of sadness and letting them rest in peace in my mind.

You felt like you were releasing a lot of grief with that balloon. Singing the songs was a great benefit, too.

Grief Responses Related to Bereaved Students ———

Death touches us. It is never easy to deal with it, and as one teacher said, It just breaks your heart. All of us are human and all of us become frightened, shocked and bewildered about what to do. The following are some of the things common in grieving students, and in grieving adults for that matter. Prolonged, they might be seen as red flags alerting you to talk to the student, parents and/or your school counselor.

Physical Response (Bodily Distress)
Headaches • Crying
Regressive changes in bowel and/or bladder control
Sleep disturbances • Restlessness
Disrupted eating patterns
Illness • Confusion
Lack of concentration
Lack of energy
Lack of attention

Emotional Responses (Feeling Reaction)
Shock • Anger/Hostility
Temper tantrums
Guilt • Sadness
Loneliness
Panic • Clinging
Withdrawal • Blame
Depression
Mood swings
Fear of being teased and rejected by classmates

Effects on Learning (Performance Reaction)
Lower grades
Absenteeism
Less productive work
Loss of interest in school and activities
Changes in peer relationships

The Bereaved Student Becoming "Super Student" ———

The results of the original study

When someone you love dies, you become a bereaved person. Bereavement causes you to feel and act differently than before the death. When this happens, it is called grief. Grief is a way you try to understand that life has changed and will never be the same again. Some students' grief means crying, not eating, being angry, withdrawing, and having problems with sleeping. School work may not get done. There may be confusion, lack of energy, and temper tantrums.

A group of bereaved students from kindergarten through grade 12 shared their experiences of being grieving students.

Student Interview ———

1. *What were your reactions to the death?*

Shocked and sad were the most common reactions. Several students, who experienced the progressive illness and death of their fathers, said they experienced shock at the time they were told their father would not live. When the actual death occurred, these students had no answer to this question; they felt it too painful to discuss. The kindergarten students said they were afraid and tried to understand what happened to their dads.

2. *What were your family's reactions to the death?*

Crying was the initial reaction. Some students told of reactions that happened several weeks after the death: the surviving parent began drinking alcohol and the siblings were perceived as not caring. Others said, each handled it alone and in their own way.

3. *What were the reactions to the death by people other than your family?*

Relatives were mentioned as reacting by crying. Friends and classmates expressed their care by telling the student they were sorry about the death; some attended the funeral. Three students did not want others to talk about the death because it was private and sad for them.

Students appreciated teachers and classmates attending the funeral. Three said they wanted to be treated normally, as if nothing had happened to them. One student had a very positive experience with a teacher. The teacher called and visited at the home, attended the funeral and provided tutorial help. She continues to check on this student although the death experience was nearly six years ago.

The Bereaved Parent

There's no mistaking the LOOK. It's stamped on the face of every newly-bereaved person, yet I failed to recognize it until I saw it on my own face in the mirror.

Parents Interview

1. *What were your reactions to the death?*

Most stated shock and disbelief. Those who experienced prolonged illness prior to death responded with being relieved and empty. Several weeks after the death, a few parents said they reacted by turning to alcohol, frivolous spending, and anger.

2. *What were your family's reactions to the death?*

Denial and evasion were reactions perceived in children and spouses. Some discussed sleep disturbances (nightmares), severe crying outbursts, sickness, and anger as additional reactions from their children.

3. *What were the reactions to the death by people other than your family?*

Relatives, friends, and neighbors were viewed as reacting with support and crying. The parents said friends took charge by making arrangements for incoming relatives and taking care of funeral procedures.

Parents said they would like to see teachers know how to help grieving students return to school and adjust because the family is in much pain and unable to help. Some suggested teachers, parents, and students have a common plan.

There are many reasons a family needs support and help from teachers:

Parents are grieving, too.

A parent is very likely to be distracted. Some may be breaking up the household of an aged parent. Others will be helping siblings or other relatives. Almost all of them will be sad, depressed, exhausted and focusing on immediate needs other than or in addition to their grieving children.

The home may be disrupted. As one eight-year-old said, *I just want us to have a happy house again*. One teen described her house as a griefpit. Guilt and anger hang on death like barnacles on a ship, so feelings at home are likely to be closer to the surface and more volatile.

We asked two mothers to write letters for us. They reflect some of the degree of stress, helplessness and also very positive cooperation.

One Parent's Letter

So many people kept pushing me to get on with my life. I know now that I just wasn't ready. These people all meant well, but that just wasn't right for me. There were too many emotions I had to work through and it took me a year and a half to become halfway human again and not dread getting out of bed in the mornings.

I was working full-time when the death occurred and when I returned to work, my concentration level was next to nothing. This brought on another problem, because from all I understood, I should have been further along in my grief at that point. I started pushing myself. I actually resented all my co-workers going through the day as if everything was the same. I finally resigned. It was really dragging me down (even though everyone told me I needed to work to take my mind off things). Then people started pushing me to socialize and get involved in volunteer work.

What I really needed to take things slower and do exactly what I wanted to do. I kept trying to please others. As I was going through all of this, I kept watching other family members. They seemed to be handling everything much better.

The children didn't talk much about going back to school. I was hurting so much for them. I didn't know how to help them. This is where the educators should come into the picture.

The whole family is working through grief and is really unprepared to help each other. I believe teachers should know how to counsel grieving students, and not just for 2 or 3 weeks, but for as long as it takes for the student to again lead a normal life (under the circumstances). I think the teachers should be trained to see when the student needs help (the student is not going to seek it out), and know how to help the student without even seeming to be doing it.

The following letter is from Dr. Lynn Bennett Blackburn. Lynn is the author of *Timothy Duck – the Death of A Friend, The Class In Room 44 and I Know I Made It Happen*. All three books deal with reactions following the death of her son, DJ, who died during his kindergarten year. We asked Lynn to tell us what the school did following DJ's death. His sister, Sarah, was enrolled in the same school.

We enrolled DJ in Kindergarten and met with the Principal and his teacher before school began to talk about his cancer and his indwelling IV line. We told them his prognosis was uncertain and promised to tell them if he recurred. His clinic nurse came to his classroom and did an inservice with his class about cancer and chemotherapy. That was the Fall of that year.

When DJ recurred in March, we let his teacher know he would be out of school and we didn't know when or if he would return. The teacher and class kept in touch with tapes and some sharing of drawings.

After some convincing on my part, the school provided DJ with homebound instruction. School is a very important part of being a child and one of DJ's biggest successes was finally doing a little beginning reading the week before he died. That same week, the school was informed that DJ was not going to survive, although we couldn't predict how soon his death would occur.

From the start of DJ's cancer, Sarah's teachers were told about his condition. I asked each of them to contact me if they saw any changes in her usual behavior at school or per- formance that persisted more than a day or two. She was blessed with incredibly sensitive, supportive teachers. Sarah told how her First Grade teacher would take her along as help- er on a trip to the office or copyroom whenever Sarah started talking a lot in class. The teacher knew that Sarah becoming a "motormouth" meant something was bothering her. During her brother's final weeks of life, school became Sarah's sense of security, her refuge from the stress at home. She counted on the normal routine there because there was no longer a normal routine at home.

DJ died in the early hours of a Saturday morning. We called one of Sarah's teachers and that teacher notified her other teacher, DJ's teacher and the administration. Sarah returned to school on Monday even though we gave her the option of waiting until after the funeral on Tuesday. Sarah was met by her teacher and given the choice of being in the room when the class was told, or waiting in the office until the teacher talked with the other students. Sarah chose to stay in class. Once the information was shared and questions answered, they got on with the normal school day.

Sarah's only other memory is that kids kept coming up and saying, "I'm sorry." She found that aggravating because in her words, "They didn't kill him or anything so why are they sorry?" I learned 3 years later that she thought she had made it happen. I think in her own way she wanted nothing at school to change because everything at home had changed.

The school was sensitive to the teachers' needs. They arranged for a substitute so Sarah's teacher could attend the funeral for Sarah's sake and so DJ's could attend for her own chance to say goodbye.

In our schools, K-6 teachers have an emphasis on feelings and expression as part of a drug prevention program. The benefit of this is that they talk about feelings related to a whole range of experiences. Children become used to sharing questions and concerns with classmates and teachers. They learn to respect each other's feelings. This gave the teacher a real advantage when DJ died. The sharing with which they had become familiar served as the avenue for tackling a difficult subject.

We also had the advantage that his death did not occur without warning. His classmates had a chance to learn about his disease when he was still "healthy." They had vocabulary the teacher could use to help them understand his death. We had time to define a good working relationship with the teachers. We didn't worry about how Sarah was doing because we had asked to be called if her behavior changed and knew the teacher would get in touch with us. We kept DJ's teacher informed so she could prepare his class and we connected her with a good resource – his clinic nurse.

Classmates

When bereaved students were asked, At school, who was the most helpful to you, the majority named their classmates.

Sixteen-year-old David is a good example. Several friends, also classmates, attended his father's funeral. After the service, they took David out to eat and to a basketball game. One special classmate-friend decided to share his father with David. They began including him in their father-son activities. David's fondest memory is how his adopted father would introduce him to others as his son. To this day, this relationship continues and David values the fatherly wisdom and attention he receives.

Not all the students had such a positive experience with their classmates. Mary, age 15, returned to school following a family member's death. The first day back, her friends turned away from her when she walked through the halls. At lunch, when she usually sat with friends and planned the weekend together, she was left to eat alone. All this added to the pain of her grieving. She began having sleep disturbances. Mary's mother became worried and helped her receive professional counseling to process her grief. She can now understand why her friends rejected her. Mary said that they could be afraid the same thing could happen to them or they probably just didn't know how to act. She wants to become a child psychologist and help bereaved students.

Mary is right. Classmates' fears often mean, this could happen to me. They don't know what to say or how to act, so they avoid their grieving friend. In this way, they are not so different from many of us adults. Also like adults, they may make upsetting comments to the grieving student as an awkward way to communicate. This is hurtful but innocent.

A kindergarten student shared one of her sad moments at school. It was nearing the Christmas holiday. Shawna's class was having art projects to make that day. They were creating gifts for their mothers and fathers. Shawna became very sad and began to cry. Happy classmates were talking about their gifts for their mommas. Her momma had been buried just three months ago. The other students have every right to be happy. It is natural for Shawna to be sad. It takes a sensitive and creative teacher to suggest another mother figure, such as an aunt or grandmother, to be the object of her gift-making.

It is normal for classmates to be awkward, frightened and concerned all at the same time. They want to help. Like us, they want to help their grieving classmate feel better. They want things normal both for their friend and themselves. Our job is to guide them in the need to be supportive, to encourage their caring and help them learn how to communicate that care and support.

Children have been known to share their care for the bereaved classmate in simple, meaningful ways. You can help them show they care by doing several things listed on the next page.

Children can show they care by:

Sending cards – perhaps drawn or made by the students during class.

Calling – or having the class talk into a tape recorder.

Visiting – you may want to make a second visit to your grieving student's home and take some of the class with you.

Taking a treat – again, made by the class or gathered by them.

There are other things you, as their teacher, can do to facilitate your class in both feelings and caring:

Express your feelings: In Dr. Lynn Bennet Blackburn's beautiful little book, *The Class In Room 44*, Ms Hall, the teacher, shares class feelings and tears after Tony, a classmate, dies:

Many children were working hard to fight back tears. Ms. Hall felt a lump in her throat, too. She encouraged them to let their tears show. "When someone dies, we have a lot of feelings," she said. "Ryan felt mixed up. Sarah felt lonely, wanting to keep reminders of Tony. Jeff is angry because what happened was unfair. Tears come with sadness, with thoughts of Tony. Can any of you use words to tell about how you feel? Can you think of what you've lost now that Tony is dead?"

Allow the children to ask questions. Children want facts and honesty. If you don't know the answer, suggest they ask their parents. They may ask about death, what happened, and about grief. Remember that every person in the world grieves at some time or another. Knowing that they can talk about subjects such as this may be one of the most precious gifts you give your class.

Encourage a return welcome. Suggesting students simply say, "I'm glad you're back." or, "It's good to see you," helps their classmate feel accepted and normal.

Encourage listening. You can suggest that students listen if their friend wants to talk. Remind them not to force talk and to not shy away from talking the way they always do – about sports, what happened at school, what they did over the week-end, etc.

Normalize sadness. You can tell them that even though sad, their classmate will be normal. Several of your children will already have experienced some type of loss – death of a pet, grandparent, divorce. Affirming that sadness is a part of life, and that even when sad people have periods of laughter and happiness gives them a valuable coping skill. They will see that they can do things that will make them fell better.

The School

Results of the original study on students and death.

When students return to school following a death, they have contact with four groups: teachers, classmates, counselors, and the administration. Most likely, the classroom teacher and classmates are most directly involved with the bereaved student. On occasion a social worker and school nurse will also be involved.

Teachers

A questionnaire of teachers' perceptions about student bereavement revealed that most felt unprepared to deal with grieving students. They shared feelings of fear and inadequacy. Those who did not have feelings of inadequacy attributed their preparedness to personal experiences with grief. However, they, too, said more information was needed about bereaved students.

Several teachers said it felt safer for them to ignore the grieving student because they did not know what to say or how to act. Other teachers advised fellow educators to keep a stiff upper lip, be firm and get the student back into the routine of being a student. Some teacher behaviors such as isolating the student, suppressing the child's need to talk, and unrealistic expectations of the student, can be harmful.

College students preparing to become teachers are not required to have any courses dealing with student crisis such as bereavement; even though facts show that **more students deal with bereavement than any other identified educational need.** In addition to formal training, we need in-service seminars, workshops and skills courses.

In the meantime, we are all concerned about how we can best support the grieving student. One parent suggested that a school conference take place soon after the bereaved student returns to school. This mother of four school-aged children recommend that the teacher, parent and student discuss a plan that all of them could follow to ease the transition back into school. With a conference, the teacher can become a vital source for the parents in observing behaviors of the child. Parents and teachers can keep lines of communication open. How the child behaves in school will give parents valuable clues to how well their child is coping.

On the other hand, a conference is not always appropriate. Another parent felt that her grief was too painful and said she would be afraid to expose her emotions during a conference. When this is the case, other alternatives can be creatively used. Written correspondence, home visits or phone calls are workable.

Sample Conference Plan for Teachers, Parents, and Students

Agenda	Sample
Welcome parent and student.	Hello (name), and welcome.
Express your care for the student.	I want to tell you that I care about your (son/daughter) (name), and the sadness you are all going through. I feel sad too, because of your (family member, i.e., father's, mother's, etc.) death.
Explain the purpose for the conference.	I invited you to this conference because I want to help (student) through this time of sadness. Sometimes when students go through a death experience, it is difficult to get back into the routine of school. It might be hard to concentrate and get your school work done; you might become very sad at times and cry. I want to help.
Assure parent and student of your help with the student's academic, social, and emotional well-being.	I can change some of your school work assignments, assign a student helper, or give you some private time. Sometimes you may even want to call home for encouragement.

Agenda	Sample
Ask student and parent for suggestions of how you might help.	Maybe you have some ideas and suggestions for me so I will know how I can better help.
Discuss the services available through school.	At our school, we have other people who care for you, too. The librarian has some books about people who have had a death in their family. The school counselor is another person who can help. If you would like to talk with the counselor or librarian about the information they have, I will arrange that.
Closing – Review the discussion, thank parent(s) and student for attending. Tell the parents that you will inform them of the student's progress in 3-4 weeks and/or the parent(s) are invited to call you at the school.	Thank you for coming and sharing with me. Hopefully, the things we've discussed will help us work together with (student's name) adjustment back to school. I will contact you, (parent's name) in 3-4 weeks to talk with you of her/his progress. Please feel free to call me here at the school if you have any concerns.

Remember to allow time for student and family to talk about what happened. This is called "framing the story" and is necessary for healing to begin.

Teachers responded to questions about how they saw and felt concerning grieving students in their class.

1. *To your knowledge have you had the experience of working with a bereaved student in your classroom?*

Responses were varied. Feelings, however, were described as inadequate and uncomfortable. Some wrote helpless, not prepared, awkward, and uncertain.

2. *Have you received any instruction on how to work with bereaved students?*

Question two received the highest number of responses negatively. Most respondents had not received any instruction. In essence, teachers expressed a need for information on working with bereavement so they can deal with grieving students.

3. *Do you feel prepared to work with bereaved students?*

For question three, those who felt prepared to work with bereaved students noted that their own personal experiences with death were most helpful. Those who did not feel prepared listed lack of experience and no instruction as their responses.

4. *Are there specific teacher behaviors needed to assist the bereaved student?*

Varied responses were given concerning teachers' behavior towards grieving students. Have a stiff upper lip, give extra help, and listen were some of the comments. However, understanding was listed several times along with patience and compassion.

5. *Do you feel there are behaviors you can anticipate from the student?*

Respondents felt there are possible behaviors demonstrated by bereaved students. Withdrawal was the most frequent response followed by anger. Other comments were also given such as, rebellious, confusion, and preoccupation.

6. *Do you feel classmates treat the bereaved student differently?*

Avoidance by withdrawing was the most common response. Some respondents explained by stating that students are not sure of what to say or how to act so it's safer to withdraw.

Do's, Don'ts and Helping

A Compassionate Friends bulletin recommended ways to be supportive of a grieving student.

> If a student seeks you out to talk, be available and really listen.
> Hear with your ears, your eyes, and your heart.
> Respect a student's need to grieve.
> Help students realize that grief is a natural and normal reaction to loss.
> Have resources available in the library about death and grief.
> Be part of a caring team by establishing communication with the parents.

Do:
Let your care and concern show.
Be available to students to talk.
Encourage them to express their grief.
Take cues from behavior that shows grieving.
Be patient and understanding: it's going to be hard to concentrate.

Touch the bereaved student. A hug or pat on the shoulder says you care.

Share your feelings with the child. It's okay to have a tear show, be sad or smile.

Acknowledge the reality that grief hurts and there are different ways to grieve.

Provide a quiet, private place to come whenever the student needs to be alone.

Help the student find a supportive peer group. Some schools have bereavement groups.

Temper your expectations of the student's performance. It's normal to be off-task.

Have resources available. Offer to read a book about grief with the student.

Keep parents informed of the child's adjustment.

Don't:

Let your sense of helplessness keep you from reaching out.

Avoid her because you're uncomfortable.

Say you know how she feels unless you too, have had the experience.

Change the subject when he mentions his dead relative.

Single out the grieving student for special privileges. She needs to be a part of the group.

You the Teacher, and Other Educators

Classroom teachers, principals, and counselors – were also interviewed in the original study.

Educators Interview

1. *Who informed you of the death in the student's family?*

Ten percent were informed of the death by other personnel. Other informants were a student, friends of the bereaved family, and the newspaper.

2. *What were your reactions?*

All felt sadness for the grieving student. Some were concerned about how they were to handle the student when he returned to school. Disbelief was described by others. Teachers who were informed of the family member's critical illness months before the death reacted by stating, no surprise, but were concerned for the student.

3. *What were your responses to the student once she returned to school?*

Most teachers welcomed the student back and offered to be available for the student should he want to talk. Others comforted the grieving student, prayed for him, and treated the student the same, as though nothing had happened.

4. *What were your responses to the classmates of the bereaved student?*

All but one teacher informed the class of the death. Several spoke with their students about their grieving classmate. They advised the students not to be overprotective and cautioned them not to discuss the bereavement unless the student initiated the subject. Some encouraged the students to comfort and console their classmate.

5. *What were the classmate's reactions toward the student once he returned to school?*

Most teachers observed the classmates as treating the grieving student as normal. Some teachers believe individual students were supportive and caring, helping their grieving friend with school work, including her in activities and writing sympathy cards. Other viewed classmates as being standoffish because they did not know how to handle the situation.

6. *Have you any education in working with bereaved students?*

Most said no. Very few received information through university courses or self-study. All felt a need for education about bereaved students and how to work with grieving students. They suggested workshops and courses. A counselor recommended role-playing through the use of scenarios to demonstrate practical methods. An administrator warned that a packaged approach could be dangerous since each death experience is unique and needs to be handled differently.

7. *What concerns do you have pertaining to school behaviors (academic, social, emotional) of bereaved students?*

Several noted they have concern about all three school behaviors and believe that a close watch on the student is essential. Others stated that bereaved students lose their motivation temporarily and cannot be expected to concentrate on schoolwork. Some experienced aggressiveness and withdrawal by bereaved students and suggested that school counselors be available for the student. Follow the normal routine was advised by a few educators; others did not observe any changes in the grieving student.

8. *What concerns do you have pertaining to school behaviors of the classmates to bereaved students?*

The greatest concern was classmates displaying inappropriate behaviors such as saying hurtful things. Teachers agreed that students need to be informed and guided in how to respond to grieving peers. Others said classmates discussed their fears about death happening to them.

9. *Are there specific behaviors, on the part of the teacher, needed to assist with the educational goals of the bereaved student?*

Continue with normal activities unless you observe changes was commented by most. Other behaviors included: take time to listen and talk, express your own grief to the student, modify school work for a time and encourage the bereaved student. A few teachers expressed the need to discern between the grieving student taking advantage of their bereavement and being responsible for learning.

10. *How can teachers assist bereaved students in achieving desired academic goals?*

The response given by most educators was listen. Others stated a need to be sensitive to the individual needs of the student. There were practical ideas: provide tutorial assistance, assign a student partner, work with the parents. Patience, concern, and understanding were other additions.

11. *What resources are available to you in working with a bereaved student?*

For many, no resources were available. Others stated the minister of their church was helpful. Some said the school's principal, other students, private and state agencies, books, faith in God, and personal experiences were good resources.

12. *Since your experience of working with a bereaved student, what recommendations do you have for your colleagues?*

Numerous responses were provided: listen to the student, be careful of what you say, let the bereaved student talk, be empathetic and compassionate, give them time to adjust, don't be afraid to talk about death, have contact with the family, prepare classmates before the grieving student returns, share your own experiences, and put your priority on observing – be alert.

Educators on all levels felt a need to establish a relationship with students before a crisis occurs. Awareness and how to deal with the bereavement process was emphasized. One teacher expressed it well. She said: *I know there are ways to help, I just didn't know how or what to do.*

Nearly everyone who is successful and happy in our world can name at least one teacher who was mentor and tutor, friend and wisdom-giver. There is one teacher who can catch a student up, engage her in the love of learning and become a person never to be forgotten. We hope you have gained from this book, and we hope that you are that one teacher many times over. We thank you for what you do.

Other helpful resources
from the Centering Corporation

Children Grieve, Too
Basic, reader friendly. Gives needed information to those who work with grieving children. Good for parents who want to know age-appropriate grief responses.

The Brightest Star
Death of a parent. Ages 5-9. Selected by the Parent Council as exceptional. Molly's mother becomes ill and later dies. She and her father go through many changes.

Animal Crackers
Death of a grandparent. Ages 5-9. Selected by the Parent Council as exceptional. Explores aging, love, illness and death.

The Butterfly Bush
Death of a grandparent. Ages 5-9. Lindsay and her grandmother plant a special butterfly bush that grows along with Lindsay. A story of love.

Remember Rafferty
Death of a beloved pet. Ages 5-11. Selected by the Parent Council as exceptional. A storybook with a unique scrapbook in the back.

A Child Remembers
A write-in journal for children ages 8-12.

Fire In My Heart, Ice In My Veins
A write-in journal for teenagers.

Reactions
A workbook for children who have experienced trauma.

Call for a complete catalog of all our available resources.

Phone: 402-553-1200

www.centering.org

QA 66. 5 LEC/
1449

Lecture Notes in Computer Science

Edited by G. Goos, J. Hartmanis and J. van Leeuwen

QMW Library

23 1164656 5

WITHDRAWN
FROM STOCK
QMUL LIBRARY

DATE DUE FOR RETURN

NEW ACCESSIONS

CANCELLED

Springer
*Berlin
Heidelberg
New York
Barcelona
Budapest
Hong Kong
London
Milan
Paris
Singapore
Tokyo*